KIDS' POWER

Healing Games
For Children Of Alcoholics

Jerry Moe and Don Pohlman

Edited by Dr. Peter Ways
Illustrations by Michelle Moe

Health Communications, Inc.
Deerfield Beac

Jerry Moe
Don Pohlman
Redwood City, California

Published by: Health Communications, Inc.
Enterprise Center
3201 S.W. 15th Street
Deerfield Beach, Florida 33442

Cover and book design by Vicki Sarasohn

About The Authors

Jerry Moe, M.A.

Jerry is the Director of Children's Services at Sequoia Hospital's Alcohol and Drug Recovery Center, Redwood City, California. He founded the Sequoia Program, The Children's Place . . . The Heart of Recovery, in February 1978. Jerry is a board member of the National Association for Children of Alcoholics. He is a national lecturer, consultant and trainer on young children of alcoholics. Jerry and his wife, Michelle, live with their three children, Josh, Aubrey and Megan, in Fremont, California.

Don Pohlman, B.A., C.A.C.

Don has worked with Jerry as a Chemical Dependency Therapist at Sequoia Hospital. He founded an innovative program for pre-school children of alcoholics at Sequoia over four years ago. Don is currently working on a Master's Degree in Somatics Psychology at Antioch University in San Francisco. He resides in Woodside, California.

Acknowledgments

This book would never have happened without the love and support of countless family members, colleagues and friends. Nancy Coxwell and Lynne Chamberlin typed the beginning stages of this project and offered valuable suggestions. Megan Tracy and Dan Foss were instrumental in computerizing the text and creating all the graphics. Their tireless support kept us moving forward. Helen Page provided many suggestions to bring greater clarity to the text.

Michelle Moe was a constant source of inspiration. Her warmth and energy are evident in her cover design and illustrations, while her support has been constant and unwavering.

Peter Ways pushed and pushed us, even at those times when we were ready to give all of it up. His feedback, suggestions and love helped to guide us. His editing was exemplary. We couldn't have done it without you, Peter!

Most of all, we'd like to thank the many young children of alcoholics who "kid tested" all of these games. Thank you for being our teachers.

Dedication

This book is dedicated to children of alcoholics of all ages.
It's not your fault;
you're not alone;
and you are truly special and beautiful kids.

Contents

Introduction

Welcome to *Kids' Power*. There is hope today for young children of alcoholics. They can and do overcome the smothering effects of an alcoholic home, and they don't have to wait until adulthood to begin this recovery. One of the most devastating illnesses known to mankind, chemical dependency progressively damages all aspects of the afflicted person: physical, intellectual, emotional and spiritual. But this is only part of the story. Alcoholism and drug addiction have a profound impact on every member of the family.

Young children are not spared; they can be deeply scarred. All of these children live in a highly chaotic and unpredictable environment, and many are subjected to neglect, physical abuse, verbal violence, inconsistency, broken promises, confusion and role reversals with their parents. Because of these traumas, children of alcoholics are at high risk for becoming juvenile delinquents, dropping out of school, running away, having unwanted pregnancies, committing suicide and developing alcoholism, drug abuse and co-dependency. Not as dramatic, but equally debilitating, are the other traits frequently exhibited by these children, such as compulsive overachieving, stress-related medical problems, difficulty in initiating and maintaining intimate relationships, inability to play and relax, and failure to take good care of self.

The self-perpetuating nature of the problem is obvious. Where does it ever stop? To avoid continuing the family legacy of alcoholism from generation to generation, prevention must involve working with young children of alcoholics — true primary prevention. It is essential to reach these youngsters to spare them from the damaging silence, isolation, pain, shame and embarrassment they endure in their homes. They must learn while they are still young that the disease is not their fault, and they are not alone. The burdens must be lifted from their shoulders.

Most attempts to reach young children of alcoholics have ultimately failed. For every program that thrives many have fallen by the wayside, often because they try to assist youngsters with tools and techniques that are only effective with adults. In a devastating manner parental alcoholism and drug abuse rob children of their childhood. Many kids must grow up way too fast by taking on adult roles and responsibilities. For others, this disease blocks the joy, creativity, spontaneity and wonder of childhood. The time has come to stop treating young children of alcoholics as if they were adults and to start treating them as children. A large part of recovery for children of alcoholics of all ages is getting in touch with that wounded child within. Play helps not only to connect with that child but also to assist in the healing process.

In the combined 15 years that we've been conducting education/ support groups for young children of alcoholics, we've stressed four primary goals: First, to help the children understand what's happening at home by teaching about chemical dependency; second, to provide a safe and supportive environment for them to freely explore and express their feelings; and third, to teach these children the skills they need to take better care of themselves and stay safe. The final goal is to simply help them be kids.

In our programs young children of chemically dependent parents can play their way to understanding and health. *Specially designed games and activities cover the following areas of critical importance: feelings, the disease of chemical dependency, family, defenses, problem solving and self-esteem (celebration of me).*

Each of these areas is represented in this book by a number of games. Most are noncompetitive and stress cooperation, trust and teamwork in an atmosphere where everyone wins. Participation in these games fosters bonding, support, laughter and recovery. Games help kids step back and look at situations with safety. They can use characters, posters and other means to express things they wouldn't feel safe expressing any other way.

We have "kid-tested" all of these games and activities with young (ages 6 to 12) children of alcoholics and addicts in a variety of settings including weekly educational/support groups, retreats, camps and workshops. We have been using some of these games for almost 10 years. Some work well with even younger children, and many are effective with adolescents and adult children of alcoholics. For each game the appropriate age group is indicated. Each writeup continues with description, example, affirmations and the materials required.

Although there are many young children who desperately need help, we don't encourage working with these youngsters solely by using this book. An effective helper needs special training and education. While many facilitators conducting education/support groups for these children are not professional therapists, nevertheless, they need quality training on an ongoing basis. Your local college or university has courses on alcoholism and chemical dependency. There are workshops and conferences offered throughout the country to provide additional training. Read thoroughly on this topic, especially about curricula designed for working with young children of alcoholics. Kids Are Special, Children Are People and Sequoia Hospital have curricula that have been tested over time. Above all, if you wish to work with these children, focus on your own personal recovery. By working on your own issues you'll truly have health to give to these needy children.

We are especially pleased to present this collection of games. There is now real hope for young children of alcoholics. As Rokelle Lerner has said, "Won't it be a great day when the words 'adult child' are no longer a part of our vocabulary because enough services are available to reach these children while they're still very young." Through education, support and love, all based primarily on play, this is gradually becoming a reality. That is *Kids' Power.*

1

Feelings

Feelings are like a thermometer — they tell what's going on inside. In a dysfunctional home the temperature is seldom comfortable because the mercury moves rapidly from rigid, cold silence to the overheated chaos of blaming, arguing and fighting. Children adapt by "shutting off" their own insides to avoid having to experience their pain and turmoil. It's important for children to identify and express a wide range of feelings, not only anger, sadness, guilt, fear and pain, but also happiness, love and joy. A liberating message for children is, "Feelings are neither good nor bad. All feelings are okay." Some feelings are more uncomfortable than others, and are painful to share with others.

Most children of alcoholics quickly learn, and learn well, the three family laws of alcoholism — Don't Talk, Don't Trust and Don't Feel. They simply don't tell the family secret to anyone. Many discount, repress and deny feelings in order to survive. It's important to be sensitive to this and move gently. These games and activities have proven to be an extremely effective way to begin reaching children. Puppets, art and stories allow children to talk and feel through play. Exploring the inner realm of feelings helps the child's world to open and initiates emotional and spiritual healing.

Games

1. Feeling Puppets

2. Twice The Dice

3. Feelings Box

4. Balloon Bash

5. Feelings Face Off

1

Feeling Puppets

(Ages 4 and up)

Children of all ages particularly enjoy working with the puppets, especially 4- to 6-year-olds. The puppets cast a magical spell on the children. They have little difficulty expressing anger, sadness, fear and guilt through the puppets.

Description

Angry Amy, Sad Sam, Fearful Frankie, Guilty Gail, Happy Harry and Confused Connie are the Feeling Puppet kids. (See examples in Figure 1.) They are sock puppets that children can easily manipulate. Each puppet has the initial of its respective feeling emblazoned on its tummy. The puppets live in a chemically dependent family. A mother and father puppet may be used interchangeably as the chemically dependent and co-dependent parents.

Using empty pop bottles to stand the puppets upright, they are placed in a semicircle. Each puppet has an identifying placard. This helps children remember their names. The group facilitators play various problems between Mom and Dad puppets in two- to three-minute sequences: confrontations about drinking and using drugs, verbal abuse, threats of divorce and family fighting. Children then pick the puppet that best represents how they would feel if they lived in the Feeling Puppet Family. They share the puppet's feelings and tell why they feel that way. Children may take turns to be more than one feeling puppet in the family.

Example

Here are some comments from 8-year-olds who recently played this game:

Confused Connie — "Why does Daddy still drink when he promised me he would stop? I don't understand."

Happy Harry — "I'm happy when Dad drinks because then I get away with murder."

Guilty Gail — "If I just could be a better kid, I know my parents would stop drinking."

Affirmations

- "All of your feelings are okay."
- "There are safe people you can talk to about your feelings."

Comments

- This is an extremely powerful activity to help children share feelings in the safety of communicating through puppets.
- Ideally, each child takes a turn with each puppet in order to share a number of feelings.

Materials

- Index card placards with the puppets' names
- Six empty pop bottles
- Eight sock puppets

Figure 1. Feeling Puppets

HAPPY HARRY

ANGRY AMY

5

Twice The Dice

(Ages 4 and up)

Children love to roll these objects of change and chance, an activity that helps create a lively and healing atmosphere. Through the die's situations and feelings come poignant memories, fostered by a fun experience that helps build trust and togetherness. This game plays well with all ages.

Description

The dice are actually plain blocks of wood, freehand lettered or stamped. One die has a family situation imprinted on its faces. Examples are: "Dad drunk," "no money," "broken promises," "parents fighting," "left alone," or "Mom blaming." The other die represents feelings: "angry," "lonely," "frightened," "happy," "confused" or "sad."

The game works best with children sitting in a circle. One child throws the dice into the middle of the circle. When the dice come to a halt, there will be a feeling and a situation facing up. The child then shares a personal experience that relates to the feeling or situation.

Example

Johnny rolled the dice. One showed "happy," and the other, "broken promise." He looked confused and frustrated. Jerry asked, "Do they match for you?" Johnny said, "No."

"Then how about happy and a promise kept?" to which Johnny readily responded and shared. Another option would have been "unhappy" and "promise broken."

Affirmations

- "It's okay for you to have strong feelings about these situations."
- "We can't always change the situations, but we can change how we react to them."

Comments

- In this activity children will often disclose their deepest secrets for the first time, thereby lessening whatever power the secrets may have.
- There will be some children who are threatened by this experience and won't want to play or share. Respect this and provide individual attention.
- Keep their environment safe.
- Be flexible — meet the needs of the child.

Materials

- Two small wooden cubes (similar to the size of dice), one with a feeling represented on each side and the other with a different situation represented on each side.

Feelings Box

(Ages 3 and up)

This game aids in the development of trust. It actively addresses feelings and problems by providing anonymity to those who cannot share openly because of trust issues. Children not only have fun playing this game, but they also have fun making it.

Description

A shoe box, old hat box or cigar box can be used. Together the children decorate the box by drawing or writing feelings on it, and pasting on feeling faces or words cut out from magazines. They can alternate between pasting, cutting and drawing.

Then the children write or draw situations in their individual lives on colored index cards. They all place their card(s) in the box. In turn, each child picks a card, reads or describes the situation, and talks about how the person may be feeling.

Example

Sally, age 9, picked a card from the Feelings Box. She described a situation where Mom never came home in time to take the kids to the movie as she had promised. Sally shared, "I feel sad and angry when my parents don't follow through with promises. It's just not fair." Other group members agreed with her and related similar experiences.

Affirmations

- "All your feelings are okay."
- "There are safe people I can talk to about my feelings."

Comments

- After each child's turn, you might want to open the discussion to more ideas and sharing.
- Sometimes children hesitate to share a feeling with the situation. Often this has to do with showing loyalty to Mom or Dad, or keeping the family secret.

Materials

- Adequate sized box
- Index cards
- Coloring materials
- Scissors
- Paste
- Magazines

Balloon Bash

(Ages 4 and up)

There is a wonderful energy created by blowing up and popping balloons. This game generates excitement and relief while helping children betray the silent "keep it to yourself" rule that's so deeply ingrained. Children love this exercise. It's upbeat, elicits enthusiasm and helps take the sting out of talking about problems and feelings that have been buried for some time.

Description

Okay, children start your balloons! The children each select a balloon, blow it up and tape it to the wall. They each take a card (index cards are good). On one side they draw or write about a problem they are having, and on the other side describe or list the feeling(s) they are experiencing with it. One by one, children volunteer to talk about their problem and the associated feeling(s). They then pop them away by sticking their balloon with a pin.

Example

Susan exclaimed, "Wouldn't it be great if problems and feelings just puffed away like magic?" The facilitator explained that most problems and feelings don't go away that fast, and that it takes talking, trying things differently, and having a lot of patience. She went on to ask, "What happens if you keep holding onto those feelings?"

Jimmy raised his hand. "It will be like blowing up a balloon — it keeps getting bigger and bigger until it explodes in your face."

"How do you feel when that happens?"

Jimmy quickly replied, "Angry and scared."

Affirmations

- "You don't have to hold onto feelings. Let them go and end their power over you."

Comments

- You can try having "active" children stand on a chair (if they choose) in front of the other kids. This helps them to sense the importance of their feelings, and to know that people will pay attention and respond to them.
- Even though the drawings by younger children on the cards may be scribbly or undecipherable to us, they hold a story. Encourage them to talk about it. You don't need to do the work for them.

Materials

- Balloons
- Index cards
- Pencils
- Colored pencils
- Pins

Feelings Face Off

(Ages 4 and up)

We have used this activity as a follow-up to a discussion on feelings and/or playing the games described earlier. It is powerful because children experience how other people's emotions and behaviors can directly affect theirs. It works best with 4- to 6-year-olds, but is effective with all age groups. It is helpful to have plenty of space and at least eight children participating. It is a good game to come back to when you are working on defenses.

Description

Divide the children equally into two groups and have them line up, facing one another about five feet apart. The facilitator designates one group as the "givers" and the other as the "takers," and then whispers the same secret feeling to each member of the "givers." On the count of three they act out the secret feeling with facial expressions and other nonverbal cues. The "takers" attempt to guess the secret feeling. After they are successful, the "takers" mirror back the facial expressions and nonverbal communication they have observed. Feedback is elicited from the "givers" about how they felt (awkward, comfortable) expressing the feeling, and from the "takers," particularly about bodily and emotional reactions to receiving the feeling.

A discussion follows about how people carry particular feelings in different parts of their bodies and how it's often difficult to guess what others are feeling when they don't talk. The children may share a time when they actually felt the particular secret feeling. Repeat this process again and again using other feelings. Rotate the "givers" and "takers" with each feeling.

Example

Jane, a "taker," was smiling spontaneously when she was met with an icy, knitted brow, curled-mouth stare from the other row. Her smile immediately changed to fright, then embarrassment, awkwardness and sadness. This was processed with Jane as she talked about her fear of Dad's anger and how she tries so hard to stay "happy."

Affirmations

- "You don't have to let other people control your feelings."

Comments

- We need to remember that children react emotionally to other people's feelings, and they can lose connection with their own identity in the process.
- Here they can begin to learn how to respond to other people from themselves rather than to constantly react to others and situations.

2
Chemical Dependency

Young children must learn that alcoholism and drug addiction are diseases, and that they hurt everyone in the family. It is particularly characteristic of alcoholism and drug addiction that the family cannot express love. With the chaos, inconsistency and unpredictability bred by chemical dependency, children are often confused. Frequent mixed messages from family members only add to their uncertainty. Children of alcoholics may fear they are going crazy because no one validates their perceptions and experiences. Sometimes it's hard to tell what's up and down anymore.

Children desperately need basic information about what is happening at home, especially in terms of drinking and/or drug-using behavior. They must learn about blackouts, addiction, relapse, denial, personality changes, enabling behavior and recovery in terms they understand. If these key concepts are clearly presented, young children can come to understand what's going on. They will come to see that their parent's drinking and using is not their fault. Moreover, they will understand that, no matter how much they would like to, they can't make it better for their parents. Such basic information may truly open the road to freedom and recovery for these children. Games and activities can help teach in a way particularly relevant to children.

Games

1. Wheel Of Recovery

2. Bicycle

3. My Poster Family

4. Crosswords To Recovery

5. Alphabet Soup

Wheel Of Recovery

(Ages 7 and up)

The "Wheel Of Recovery" combines the fun of a television game show with learning about the key concepts of addiction and taking care of yourself. The wheel — with different game inserts such as defenses, family, feelings and chemical dependency — helps children to stop denying their pain and begin recovery.

Description

A rotating wheel similar to the one seen on "The Wheel of Fortune" is used. The wheel has individual slots with numbers in each area. There is also a pegboard with hidden placards that contain secret messages. An example is: "It's not my fault."

Children can be divided into two teams (stressing cooperation and teamwork) or play individually. In team play, each team chooses a name for themselves. One child spins the wheel, another is time keeper and a third exchanges the play money. A card selector is also needed. A panel of judges is optional.

The wheel is spun. The number on which it stops is the number of dollars the individual or team will receive if they answer correctly. If the question is missed, the money goes to the other team or into the pot. If the question is answered correctly, the individual or team picks a letter on the pegboard. If they guess the letter correctly, they can attempt to guess the phrase or move on and spin again. If they guess the letter or phrase wrong, play reverts to the other team. Play continues until someone guesses the phrase and wins the bonus.

During presentations, we invite adult members of the audience to participate. They are asked to list and describe symptoms that distinguish chemical dependency from social drinking. As they brainstorm the answer, time expires, the horn sounds and the children then answer the questions, win the money and get the bonus.

Affirmations

- "It's important that you help each other."
- "It's okay not to know all the answers."
- "You don't need to always be right. It's okay just to have fun."

Comments

- Children sometimes become very competitive. Use the affirmations to encourage teamwork.
- With this game children have a lot of fun while learning about the disease, learning they have choices and developing important social skills and relationships.

Materials

- Cardboard
- Spinner
- Felt-tip pens
- Play money
- Pegboard and hooks
- Bell, whistle or foghorn
- Questions about alcoholism and addiction

Be creative. From the cardboard make a wheel and attach the spinner (see Figure 2). Placards, to be hung on the pegboard hooks, can be made from 6x6-inch cardboard squares and lettered brightly with colored felt-tip pens (see Figure 3). The timekeeper will need the bell, whistle or foghorn. Have fun!

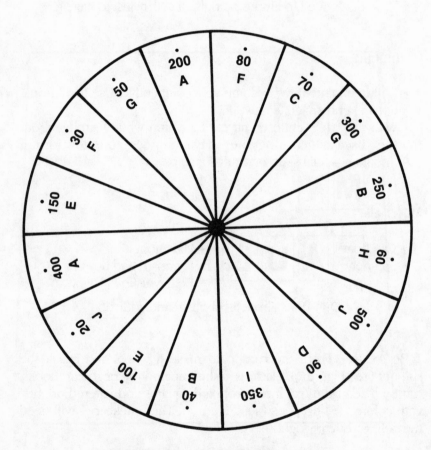

Figure 2. The Wheel of Recovery

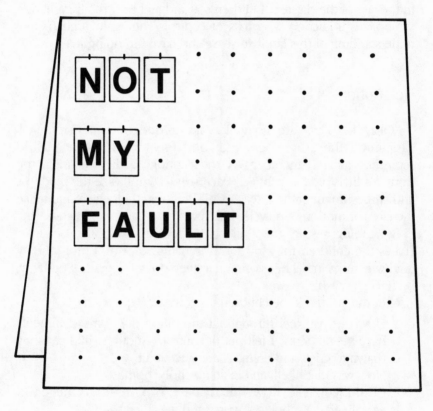

Figure 3. Wheel of Recovery Pegboard

Bicycle

(Ages 4 and up)

This exercise provides children with a hands-on experiential process that not only captures their imagination but also focuses on the reality of the disease. Children see and feel how the bicycle ride symbolizes addiction with loss of control. They gain fundamental understanding of this family disease and have fun doing it.

Description

"Okay kids, we are going to take a ride on our octocycle!" (assuming there are eight kids and eight chairs). Each child represents a family member with the alcoholic/addict steering at the front. An invisible bar connects each seat to emphasize the rigidness and enmeshment of the disease. Children sit in their chairs and make the circular motion of bicycle pedals with their arms and hands.

By reading a story (see "Bicycle Ride Narrative") the facilitator "takes the children for a ride." An initially peaceful, joyful journey gradually turns into a rainstorm on a steep downhill grade. Suddenly, no brakes! Crash!

After the crash ask the children the following questions:

1. How did you feel throughout the bike ride? Some comments have been: "Scary. I felt out of control." Another child certainly drawn to crisis and drama stated, "Exciting."
2. How was that like living in an alcoholic home?
3. Could you see how the disease progresses? One child exclaimed, "Yeah, it got worse and we all crashed!"
4. Was it your fault? No, it's not your fault.
5. Where can you go to get help?
6. If the alcoholic gets back on the bike, does that mean you have to? Each time this is asked a chorus of "no's" echoes loudly.

Example

See the questions above. Nine-year-old Danielle summed it up best. "The bike ride was fun at first but scary at the end. Alcoholics don't have brakes when it comes to drinking. I guess relapse is when they think they have brakes even though they don't."

Affirmations

- "You don't have to go on the alcoholic ride. You can get help."
- "You can make helpful choices to stay safe."
- "It's not your fault; you don't have to be alone anymore."

Comments

- The exercise also helps children bring the disease to conscious reality by talking about feelings.
- Learning the disease is not their fault and brainstorming ways of taking care of themselves are made possible by this game.

Materials

- Bicycle Ride Narrative
- Chairs

Bicycle Ride Narrative

"Okay, everybody in position.

"We are going for a nice ride through the country. It's a beautiful day. The sun is out and the grass is green. There's no wind, just a gentle warm breeze. We are pedaling slowly, breathing evenly, enjoying the scenery, and chatting and laughing with each other. We put on the brakes slowly as a dog wags his way across our path.

"As we are gathering speed, a few dark clouds begin to appear over the horizon and the breeze becomes a little more stiff as the smooth pavement turns into a dirt road. We begin to pedal a little harder and grab onto the handlebars a little tighter. The clouds are becoming darker and some light rain begins to fall as the dirt road is getting slippery and bumpy. We keep putting on the brakes while still moving. We have to lean forward and pedal harder as we are going up a hill. Our legs and stomach are sore as our hands grab the handlebars even tighter. The rain is coming down harder and at times the bike almost tips over.

"We reach the top of the hill exhausted but it is raining so hard we have to keep moving. We start pedaling faster as we go down the other side of the hill. The rain is slapping harder onto our faces. The bike is sliding back and forth across the road. Loud sounds of thunder can be heard. Lightning strikes a tree near us. We are pedaling faster and faster, and holding on tighter and tighter. Our feet keep slipping off the pedals as we go faster and faster. Skipping and sliding, we try the brakes. The brakes don't hold — they no longer work. We're losing control. Pedals are spinning faster and faster. The road is much steeper and bumpier as we go faster and faster, trying the brakes (no brakes) and holding on for dear life. CRASH — the bike tips over."

Bicycle Questions

1. What was that like for you?
2. How was this like alcoholism/addiction?
3. How was this like what you experience in your own home?
4. Was everyone affected?
5. When you fell down, who did you have to help first?
6. What would you do if the alcoholic/chemical dependent wanted to get back on the bike and continue down the hill?
7. Whose fault is it?
8. Where can you go to get help?

"Okay, since your family cycle is all busted up we have a new cycle for each of you."

My Poster Family

(Ages 4 and up)

This is an especially good game for young children who haven't developed sophisticated verbal skills. It is a powerful window into the child's world. Since it doesn't necessarily require any verbal sharing, this game is less threatening than talking might be. It embodies the principle that a picture can be worth more than a thousand words.

Description

Spread crayons, colored markers and pencils on the floor throughout the room. Give each child two pieces of colored poster board. The facilitator asks the children to draw a picture about family situations involving drinking and using other drugs. Ask them to show: (1) the part that alcohol and drugs play in their family; (2) the way they see themselves in the family; and (3) the problems they face at home — parental drinking, fighting, no one paying attention to them, confusion and anything else that feels important.

From the start, let the children know they don't have to share their drawings with anyone. Encourage the children to be creative and do two pictures if they'd like. Facilitators should roam around the room, spending some time with each child in the group. It is important to let the children explain their pictures instead of your trying to analyze them. When everyone is finished, ask for volunteers to share their pictures with the group. Use this opportunity to introduce basic facts about addiction, such as personality changes, denial and blackouts. Follow with a group discussion.

Example

A 9-year-old girl poignantly portrayed her family's suffering. She drew an oversized liquor bottle, with arms and legs, running across the page. On the stem of the bottle was a hideous face. Chasing after the bottle was her alcoholic father. His hair was askew, and his face expressed panic. One hand was about to seize the bottle. Behind Dad was Mother. One hand was reaching for Dad's collar to prevent him from snatching the bottle. Tears filled her eyes. Behind Mom were the girl and her little brother running so as not to be left behind. They looked sad and scared. In describing her picture, the little girl said, "I'm tired. I don't want to keep running around anymore. Why can't all this stop right now?"

Affirmation

- "You are a special, creative person."

Comments

- This activity is a powerful tool to begin reaching children. It's important to stress that there isn't a right or a wrong way to do this activity. This gives kids more freedom to communicate their family situation. Even the scribbles of preschoolers have a definite story behind them.
- Give the children an opportunity to share their story, first privately, then with the group. Provide each one a chance to be heard and validated.

Materials

- Poster board
- Crayons
- Colored markers
- Colored pencils

Crosswords To Recovery

(Ages 10 and up)

This exercise utilizes a stimulating, thought-producing crossword puzzle that focuses on basic concepts of alcohol and drug addiction.

Description

There are two principal ways to play this game (with some groups one may work better than the other):

Method #1: Provide individual crossword sheets for each child. When everyone is finished, review and discuss the correct solution. This method has a conventional classroom atmosphere to it.

Method #2: This involves more action and higher energy. The facilitator draws the blank puzzle on the board and encourages the entire group to participate in its solution. Children become actively involved in brainstorming the answers.

Example

See next page.

Affirmations

- "Your life can improve despite the alcoholism and addiction in your family."
- "You don't have to be perfect to get approval."

Comments

- Be aware of competition and put-downs, as well as children needing to be right. Stress cooperation and group effort.
- This game helps children learn more about the key concepts of addiction.

Materials

- Appropriate age sensitive crossword puzzle(s)
  (See sample on the next page.)

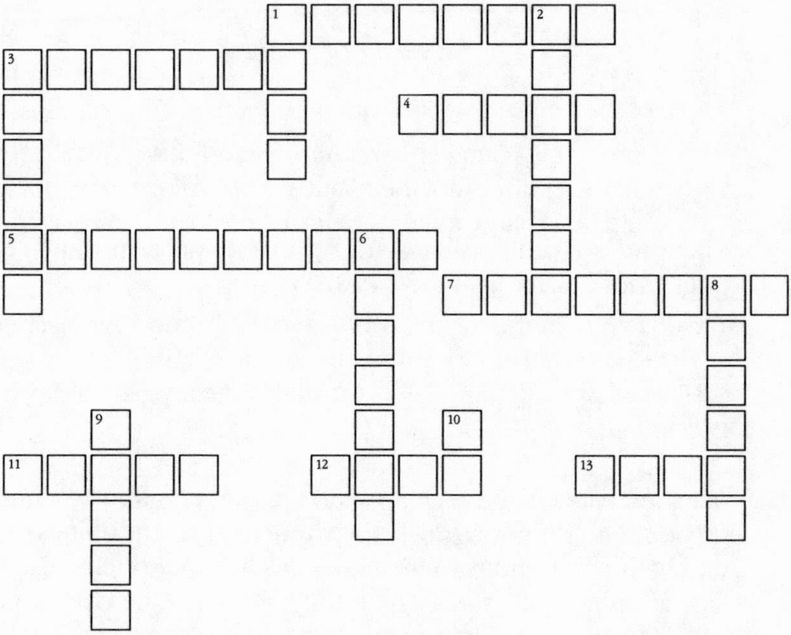

Across

1. When the family gets better
3. Alcoholism is a _____
4. The drinking is not the kids' _____
5. A disease where a person can't stop drinking
7. All my _____ are okay
11. Alcoholics can recover but they are _____ cured
12. Remember to always stay _____
13. A parent's drinking can _____ children

Down

1. I can be _____ with people I trust
2. When an alcoholic starts drinking again
3. Pretending something isn't a problem
6. I am _____
8. When parents get drunk kids sometime feel _____
9. Alcoholism hurts _____ person in the family
10. The most important person is _____

Figure 4. Crosswords into Recovery

Answers:

Across — (1) recovery, (3) disease, (4) fault, (5) alcoholism, (7) feelings, (11) never, (12) safe, (13) hurt
Down — (1) real, (2) relapse, (3) denial, (6) special, (8) guilty, (9) every, (10) me

Alphabet Soup

(Ages 6 and up)

This game helps young children understand that alcoholism/drug addiction in the family is not their fault. It's one thing when they know this in their heads and quite another when they realize it in their hearts. This game helps them do that. Although "Alphabet Soup" stands well by itself, it usually works best as an adjunct to another game or activity in the Alcoholism/Chemical Dependency section.

Description

The "Alphabet Soup" sheet (see Figure 5) is given to all group members. The 4 C's are read one at a time, and the meanings of each C and their applications to the children's lives are briefly discussed. A similar process takes place with the 5 S's. Then the children color their "Alphabet Soup" sheet with crayons or colored markers. Have them draw a picture illustrating that the drinking/drug use at home really isn't their fault.

If time permits, have the kids cut out pictures and words from magazines to illustrate the 4 C's and 5 S's. They can make collages using large poster board illustrating how they can't stop or start their parent's alcoholism/drug abuse. These collages may be hung on the wall during group meetings to remind children that it's not their fault.

Example

Eight-year-old Ben broke into tears when he realized that his dad's alcoholism was not his fault. It was probably the sixth or seventh time he had played "Alphabet Soup." As tears streamed down his face, he said, "You really mean it's not me. I'm not a bad boy that can't do anything right. I am not the bad one. No, it's not my fault." Everyone clapped and cheered for Ben. Something like this doesn't happen every time "Alphabet Soup" is played, but each time, young children get closer to understanding that it's not their fault.

Affirmations

- "You are a special person filled with goodness."
- "It's okay to take good care of yourself."
- "You are the most important person in the world."

Comments

- If at all possible, do include the option of making the collages. Hang them on the wall during subsequent sessions with the children. They will provide a visual reminder to the kids that it's not their fault and they can't affect chemical dependency.
- Near the end of each session with the children, review "Alphabet Soup." Repetition reinforces the memory of these facts.

Materials

- "Alphabet Soup" sheets   • Colored markers/crayons

(For optional activity — poster board, magazines, scissors and glue)

It's important for kids from alcoholic homes to remember the **4 C's** and the **5 S's**.

The 4 C's

I didn't **CAUSE** the alcoholism.
I can't **CONTROL** it.
I can't **CURE** it.
But I can learn how to **COPE** with it.

The 5 S's

I didn't **START** the alcoholism.
I can't **STOP** it.
I don't have to **SUFFER** with it.
I don't have to feel **SHAME** because of it.
I can **SAVE** myself in spite of it.

Figure 5. Alphabet Soup

3

Family

Alcoholism and drug addiction hurt all members of the family. Denial and delusion block honest communication among family members, and parents seldom meet their children's physical and emotional needs consistently. As a result, children feel alone in their families. Beset by the unpredictability and inconsistency of addictive disease, everyone in the family simply tries to survive. This is no small feat when you are living with alcoholism and chemical dependency.

It's important for children to understand that chemical dependency affects the behavior of the alcoholic/addict, as well as everyone else in the family. They can learn that everyone in afflicted families needs support and assistance, especially themselves. They need a safe place to talk about what's happening in their families, as well as the opportunity to share their feelings about it. Above all, they find that many other children live in similar environments with the same problems. In this way they will realize that they don't need to be alone anymore.

Games

1. Bubblegum Family

2. Totem Pole Family

3. Family Collage

4. My Family Masterpiece

5. Family Sculpture

Bubblegum Family

(Ages 6 and up)

In a simple yet powerful way, Bubblegum Family helps children understand what happens to everyone in a family with alcoholism and chemical dependency. We frequently use this game as a demonstration during community education sessions on working with young children of alcoholics. Often adults also participate. Children of all ages learn and have fun with this game.

Description

Almost everyone has had some experience chewing bubblegum. What's your favorite brand? Remember how sticky it becomes after a few quick chews if you take it out of your mouth? Yuck! Have you ever had the pleasure of getting a great wad stuck on the bottom of your shoe?

In this game everyone imagines there are 9,997 pieces of slightly chewed bubblegum in an imaginary circle on the floor. Children volunteer to role play an addicted parent, the spouse and several children. Using a narrative, the facilitator orchestrates a scenario in which everyone in the family gets stuck in the addiction (bubblegum).

First the addicted parent gets stuck by using alcohol and drugs. Then the spouse and children get stuck in their attempts to help the addicted parent. Once stuck in the gum everyone has a hard time moving around. They lose choice in what they think and do. Only by taking good care of themselves first can family members get unstuck. Different strategies for taking good care of self and the progression of the disease are stressed.

Example

This activity allowed Jim, age 12, to understand how he impedes his mother's recovery by constantly taking care of her. Jim and three others played the roles of his father and siblings. Jim's mom was stuck in the center, and the rest of the family got stuck trying to help her. We instructed Jim and the others to circle very closely around his "mom." Then we asked Mom to come out of the bubblegum. Jim said, "Even if she wanted to, she couldn't move because everyone else is in the way trying to take care of her. Boy, I guess it's true that if I take care of me, I give Mom the space to do the same for herself. I think I understand it now, but it's hard to let go of her. I guess it begins with me."

Affirmations

- "You can trust your feelings to help you know what's best."
- "It's okay to take good care of yourself."

Comments

- Allow children the opportunity to role-play various family members. This lets them see how everyone becomes stuck in the same way.
- Process feelings and discuss how this exercise is similar to their own family experiences.

Materials

- Bubblegum Family Narrative

Bubblegum Family Narrative*

"We're going to do an activity now called Bubblegum Family. Almost everyone's had an experience chewing bubblegum. Whether your favorite bubblegum is Hubba Bubba, Carefree, Bazooka or Bubble Yum bubblegum, there are all different kinds of bubblegum that people chew.

"You know how someone can chew bubblegum for about 30 seconds and then take it out of his or her mouth. How does it feel? Sticky! It's real sticky and yucky. Here in the middle of the floor is an imaginary circle. We've stayed up the last 24 hours, and chewed piece after piece of bubblegum, all for 30 seconds. We've then thrown it into our imaginary circle. Here in this circle are 9,997 pieces of slightly chewed bubblegum.

"Here we have a family. 'Miss, please come up.' I want you to meet Tammy. She is 35 years old, a mother of three, a wonderful mom. She has a full-time job. Just an incredible lady. Since she's been a young adult, Tammy goes out each weekend and drinks with her friends, but it doesn't seem to be a problem. All of a sudden as Tammy's going through life, she steps right in the bubblegum. All of a sudden she's stuck. 'Try to move, Tammy.' "

"Well I'm trying, but I can't really move too much."

"That's right, you can't move too much. That's addiction. People get stuck. Watch Tammy. She can sway from side to side. She really thinks she's not stuck, that she can get out of that real quickly, but she can't.

"What happens as time goes on is that Tammy becomes more and more preoccupied with the gum while she's stuck in it. She can't do as good a job at work. She's out sick a lot. She can't be as productive because she's preoccupied with the gum. It's really starting to slow her down. She doesn't have freedom of choice anymore. When it comes to her kids, she can't take care of them like she used to. She's trapped in that gum. She's stuck! She doesn't have as much choice as she had before. She's not spending as much time with her kids. She prepares dinner and just goes off on her own.

"Tammy has a husband named Fred. Fred loves his wife very much. Fred's been very concerned about Tammy. 'Haven't you, Fred?' "

"Why, yes."

"Fred has been concerned because he notices his wife is stuck in the gum. She's on probation at work because she has been absent so many days. Her last review wasn't very good. Fred has noticed over the last few months that he has had to take on more and more of the responsibilities at home. He's starting to prepare dinner. Fred is also spending time helping the kids with their homework and helping them with their projects on the weekend. He's very concerned about his wife. He doesn't get to spend as much time with her alone because she seems preoccupied and distant. She's just stuck in that gum.

"Because Fred cares and loves his wife, what do you suppose he tries to do? He tries to free his wife from the bubblegum. 'So go ahead, Fred, go and try to help your wife.'

"As Fred tries to help his wife, all of a sudden he gets stuck in the bubblegum. Now Fred is stuck. 'Try to move around, Fred.' Notice, he thinks he can move around and he thinks he's free, but he's really stuck. Remember that addiction is a progressive disease. When Tammy first got stuck, the gum only went up to her calf. Now when Fred is stuck with her, it comes all the way up to just above their knees! So how does this affect Fred? He's preoccupied at work. He's thinking about having to come home and prepare meals. He wonders if she is going to be drunk or sober. Will she embarrass him at the dinner party next week? He can't be as productive at work. He thinks more and more about her. He's not available to his kids on a consistent basis anymore. He's not always helping them with their homework. Fred is even beginning to drink with her sometimes. So all of a sudden he's stuck.

"We then have the oldest child, Jimmy. Jimmy's very concerned because not only is Mom stuck, but Dad's stuck. Neither one is there for him on a consistent basis. Out of love and concern, he tries to help them get unstuck. As Jimmy goes and tries to get his parents unstuck, look what happens. In an attempt to help, he gets stuck in the gum. How does this affect Jimmy? His life isn't as free.

"How does this happen? Jimmy has a hard time concentrating in school. He thinks about having to go home to take care of a younger brother and sister. He's thinking about whether or not he should bring friends home. He might get embarrassed by what's happening there. He's real concerned. Jimmy doesn't have very many opportunities to play anymore because he's taking care of his younger brother and sister. When he does have a chance to play, he's often worried about Mom and Dad. He might be yelled at for something he didn't do.

"As younger brother and sister attempt to help Mom, Dad and older brother get unstuck from the bubblegum, they will get stuck too. The entire family gets stuck. That's the Bubblegum Family. Why do the kids get stuck? It's real important. Why do kids get stuck in the bubblegum? They get stuck because they try to help their parents first. So if the reason why kids get stuck is because they try to help, how do kids get unstuck? Kids get unstuck when they stop trying to take care of other people in their family, like Mom, Dad, brothers or sisters. They can begin to take good care of themselves. That's how kids get unstuck from the bubblegum.

"What does it mean to take care of yourself? What different ways can kids take good care of themselves? Go out and play. Talk to a teacher. Ask a counselor for help. Go to a neighbor's house. Call Grandma if there's a mess at the house and you don't want to be there. These are some of the different ways kids can take care of themselves.

"Notice how everyone attempted to help Mother. They were all around her. Everyone got stuck in the bubblegum. Even if Mom wanted to get unstuck, she couldn't! There's no room for her to get out. The family has blocked her path to recovery. Kids need to take care of themselves.

"We have to remember that recovery takes time. There might be a time when Jimmy gets unstuck and starts to take good care of himself, but two weeks from now there will be a big dinner party at the house with Dad's business associates. Mom is still stuck in the bubblegum, so Jimmy might have to go do all the preparations.

"Recovery is a process. We take two steps forward and because we're human, sometimes we take a step backward. So we get stuck and unstuck. We get stuck and unstuck.

"I am 32 years old. When I was a teenager, I was so stuck in bubblegum that it came up to my neck. I have been in recovery for a long time now. I don't have bubblegum up to my neck anymore. I still have bubblegum, but now it's bubblegum from about the ankle down. That's why I stay in recovery to help me get off the rest of that bubblegum.

"That's the Bubblegum Family."*

*The narrative was transcribed from an actual training done by Jerry Moe in July, 1987.

Totem Pole Family

(Ages 6 and up)

In this game, children learn cooperation, sharing and together-ness. It emphasizes their common bond while encouraging their uniqueness. It also offers an opportunity to blend their artistic impressions, feelings, thoughts, memories and play experience together to more fully understand themselves, the disease and their own recovery.

Description

Working in small teams, children select a cardboard grocery box from an available supply. Each team is assigned to make an Alcoholic Family member or a Recovering Family member. Then they decorate the boxes with paint, beads, buttons, yarn, pine cones and other available items. Some children carefully and intensely construct their family member's head and face; others have fun just talking about kids' stuff while they work.

When the children finish their artistic expressions, they assemble them on the Alcoholic Family or Recovery Family totem by making holes in the top and bottom of their box and sliding it on the appropriate pole. Then each team describes its family members, and their feelings and thoughts while doing the work. If time permits, the children are asked to go to the pole of their choice. Usually they all run to the Recovery Family pole with shouting and cheering. Anyone who goes to the Alcoholic Family pole is soon persuaded to join the Recovery Family.

Example

Janice pursed her lips, knitted her brow and excitedly exclaimed, "Why don't we add a few more buttons to curl the mouth up so she looks even angrier?" This triggered a memory and she proceeded to tell the facilitator about the time her mom was drinking and yelling at her for no reason at all, and about how angry and scared she had become.

Affirmation

- "It's okay for you to feel and to ask for help."

Comments

- If any children do go to the Alcoholic Family pole in the last stage of the game, it's important to emphasize that staying in an alcoholic family may be unavoidable.
- Stress that even in an alcoholic family they can choose recovery and grow to feel better about themselves.

Materials

- Cardboard cartons and boxes
- Paints
- Brushes
- Glue
- Buttons
- Yarn
- Two poles
- Other decorative materials

Family Collage

(Ages 8 and up)

We use this activity to show what happens to alcoholic and chemically dependent families. Because this game doesn't necessarily require kids to share verbally, it permits a less threatening introduction to the topic. Like "My Poster Family," page 24, it provides a powerful window for facilitators to enter the children's world.

Description

Spread a variety of magazines on the floor. Give each child a pair of scissors, poster board and glue. Have the children look through magazines for words and pictures that tell the story of themselves and their families. Then have them cut out their "finds" and paste them on poster board in any fashion they choose. The facilitators give the children ideas and suggestions.

It is important to spend time with each child individually. If they wish, let the children describe the story of their collage. Don't interpret it for them. Once all have finished, ask for volunteers to share their work with the group. Subsequent discussion then emphasizes how alcoholism and chemical dependency hurt everyone in the family.

Example

The children quietly talk and joke during the cutting and pasting activity. Everyone searches for liquor and smoking advertisements because these pictures dominate the collages. As they work the children realize that they share similar experiences. Ten-year-old Kurstine summed it up best, "I never thought so many kids had the problem in their family, too. It helps to talk about it. I'm not the only one. That makes me sad and happy at the same time."

Affirmations

- "Your creations are very special."
- "It's good to talk about your problems."
- "You are not alone."

Comments

- It is essential to have a wide variety of magazines depicting people of different racial and cultural groups.
- Encourage creativity and variation not only in terms of what they cut out but also how they place it on the poster board.
- Stress that there is no right or wrong way to do this game. This relieves any anxiety children may face about doing it perfectly. Let them know that their creations are indeed very special.
- Above all, allow children to tell you the story of their collage. It's fine to ask questions, but let them tell you what it means. Only in this way may you truly begin to enter their world.

Materials

- Wide variety of magazines
- Scissors
- Glue
- Poster board

My Family Masterpiece

(Ages 3 and up)

This game offers children a hands-on, tactile experience that helps to revive hidden memories, emotions and thoughts by bringing them to conscious awareness and reality.

Description

Using Styrofoam cups, Popsicle sticks, colored markers for making faces, and/or Tinker-toys, the kids create their own three dimensional family model. If anyone gets stuck, it often helps to suggest specific family scenes: family watching TV, going to the movies, sitting at the dinner table, etc.

Example

One child, Dianne, looked perplexed and resistant. Don asked if she was having trouble doing the game. She said, "Yeah, my family never does anything together."

"Well," said Don, "you're all in the same house together." A light went on, and then she used the Tinker-toys to make separate rooms; after putting faces on the Styrofoam cups, she situated each figure in a separate room. Don said, "It looks really lonely there." Dianne nodded, finally able to tell how each person reacted to Dad's drinking and was either spending time alone or arguing and blaming each other.

Affirmations

- "You are becoming more aware of your feelings."
- "It's okay for you to feel them and to think about them. It helps you to grow and to know."

Comments

- As a prelude to this activity, spend time discussing the various kinds of families children may live in: nuclear, foster, extended, blended, separated, divorced, gay or adopted families.
- Stress to children that all kinds of families have special qualities. All families are special.

Materials

- Tinker-toys
- Styrofoam cups
- Popsicle sticks
- Colored markers

Family Sculpture

(Ages 6 and up)

In this game children gain a sense of power from positioning their silent "family members" and involving the characters in whatever interactions they wish. They love it. Nobody resists, ignores, argues, blames or shames. The kids have control in a nonthreatening situation.

Description

Each child takes a turn in creating a Family Portrait. They choose other members of the group to represent members of their family and position them to create a family scene. The actors must remain silent while the "sculptor" describes the various family members and directs how they interact with one another. He or she may also interact with them verbally or nonverbally, but they must continue to remain silent. After each child's scenario, there is group discussion.

Example

A favorite setting is the dinner table. Tammy, age 10, placed her actors appropriately, strolled slowly around the table, and stopped first next to her dad. "I'm tired of your sitting here every night ordering everyone around!" she exclaimed. "Who do you think you are?" All the children laughed and clapped. Then she walked up to Mom, stared at her coldly and said, "And you. I can't stand it when you try to please him all the time and make excuses for him. It makes me sick."

Affirmations

- Some are tailored to the specific sculpture and its interactions. In the example given above: "It's okay for you to let people know when you're angry."
- Others involve all the children: "Alcoholics can and do recover," "It's not your fault," and "You need and deserve help for yourself."

Comments

- This psychodrama helps the child acknowledge parental alcoholism and drug addiction.
- Also it can be a critical exercise in reclaiming personal power, understanding feelings, and learning healthy ways to deal with difficult situations.

4

Defenses

Defenses are behaviors and habits that protect us from pain and difficult feelings. They are like masks or armor hiding us from others and often from ourselves. Defenses are neither good nor bad. They help children of alcoholics survive in the highly chaotic and unpredictable chemically dependent family. Some children may be highly dependent on them to survive. Therefore, it is essential to respect a child's defenses and not threaten them. They are an important part of the child's repertoire for coping with inconsistency and craziness.

While it's important not to threaten children's defenses, it is equally important to help them become aware of their defenses. Only then are they able to choose when to defend themselves and when to become vulnerable. There are times when it's imperative for children to raise defenses, e.g., when being confronted by a stranger, or when experiencing a verbal tirade by a drunk parent. There are other times when raising defenses may be counterproductive. Our job is to help children become aware enough so that they can begin to choose how they will respond to situations and people. Given choices they may decide to risk new behaviors. In this way they add to their repertoire of responses in the world.

Games

1. Sno White And The Seven Defenses

2. Line Of Defense

3. Defense Mate

47

Sno White And The Seven Defenses

(Ages 10 and up)

"Oh no, oh no, the alcoholic woes." The Seven Defenses live with Sno White who is chemically dependent. Each of the seven uses a particular defense to hide his or her pain and frustration about living in such a chaotic family. Blaming, Perfect, Clowning, Rebelling, Talking a Lot, Quiet and Crying all put on masks to shield themselves. How do they really feel about what's happening at home? What happens when they find a bottle of booze?

Adolescents and adults especially enjoy this game. We very often let younger children be a part of the "audience." This allows them to hear the story and participate in the follow-up discussion on defenses.

Description

Since reading from a script is an integral part of this game, it's important to be sensitive to the children's reading abilities. The facilitator chooses one child to play Sno White and seven children to play the various defenses. Each of the seven gets an identifying placard and a two-page script. The children read and act out the script, which includes a singing rendition of "Oh no, oh no, the alcoholic woes," and then the scenario is discussed by the players and the audience.

Members of the audience are asked to name those with whom they particularly identified. The facilitators may then give a simple definition of defenses and basic information about this topic, and ask questions of the children about the various defenses they use in their own lives. "Oh no, oh no, the alcoholic woes."

Example

This activity has worked well in Parenting in Recovery groups. Gloria, a 35-year-old adult child now married to a practicing alcoholic, played Blaming in a recent group. Halfway through the two-page script she broke. into tears. Afterwards she said, "I saw myself in a way I never have before. How did you know my whole life's been about blaming? I'm always the martyr. I blame my dad, husband and children for my present condition. It gets me nowhere. Blaming doesn't work. I think I'm starting to get it. Why does it take so long?"

Affirmations

- "You can trust your feelings to help you know."
- "It's okay to take good care of yourself."

Comments

- Let children take turns playing the various defenses but remember that reading ability is required.
- In the follow-up discussion let children know that all defenses are okay. Help them become aware of the defenses they use in various situations.
- Without attempting to take away their defenses, encourage them to take risks and check out other behaviors.
- Help them differentiate between those situations where it's essential to raise their defenses and where it's safe to lower them. In this way they will begin to have more choice in how they respond to situations and people.

Materials

- Scripts
- Placards for identifying each defense

Sno White And The Seven Defenses Narrative

Chorus:

"Oh no, oh no, the alcoholic woes (*whistle*) oh no, oh no, oh no.
Oh no, oh no, the drug abuse woes (*whistle*) oh no, oh no, oh no.
Oh no, oh no, the alcoholic woes (*whistle*) oh no, oh no, oh no.

Oh no."

Blaming: "Just look at this house. It's a garbage dump. Dirty dishes, plates and newspapers are all over the place. Sno White is using alcohol and cocaine again. She really doesn't care about it. She doesn't care about us. That lady is destroying my life. It's all her fault."

Perfect: "Calm down now. Here, I'll take care of picking up this mess. Don't get so upset. We just have to be strong. It's like the straight A's I got on my last report card. You just have to keep working very hard and never, never give up. Let me take over. I'll fix things."

Clowning: "Hey, how about this one, smarty pants? How many feet in a yard? No, not three. It depends on how many people are in the yard. Yuk, yuk, yuk. Burned your face." (*Make a funny face.*)

Rebelling: "You're nuts if you expect me to clean up this dump. Hey man, it's not my mess. With the way Sno White always treats us, drinking and using drugs, why should I care? I'll fix her. I ain't gonna try in school anymore. Getting bad grades will hurt her. I'll get even. Hey, Quiet, you with me?"

Quiet: (*Frowns and hides behind other kids.*)

Perfect: "You can't do that. You must get good grades so you can go to an excellent college. Even if you start cutting school,

I'll tutor you. Just let me take care of it. I'll fix everything for you. I know exactly what to do."

Rebelling: "Hey, **stuff it, bookworm**."

Blaming: "And you wonder why Sno White drinks and uses drugs. And you wonder why this house looks like a city dump. It's all your fault. You guys are always fighting. You guys are always yelling and screaming. You make Sno White drink and use drugs."

Crying: "Sob, sob, sob." (*Make a low-pitched crying sound.*)

Blaming: Turn off the waterworks. It's all your' fault, too. Just **shut up**.

Talking A Lot: "**Hold it.** Did you know Mount McKinley is the tallest mountain in the western United States? Jimmy Brum barfed this morning during math class, and we had mashed potatoes and gravy in the cafeteria for lunch, and the Smurf's Special is on TV this Thursday night, and Jimmy Brum barfed again after mashed potatoes and gravy in the cafeteria, and . . ."

Crying: "Sob, sob, sob." (*Make a low-pitched crying sound.*)

Blaming: "Now look what you've done, motor mouth. She's crying all over again. It's all your fault. What's wrong with you? You know her best friend is Jimmy Brum. It's all your fault."

Clowning: "And now for this late-breaking news flash — boy kills himself. He drowns in his own tears. Four others stranded. They floated away in the flood. Film at 11. Yuk, yuk, yuk." (*Make a funny face.*)

Talking A Lot:	"Every 20 minutes someone in the United States dies of drowning. Most of these people weren't wearing life jackets. The 49ers won the last Superbowl by the smallest winning margin ever. Next Friday our class will be going on a special field trip to the Phillips' Caverns. Tomorrow night for dinner we've gonna have pepper pizza. I just can't wait."
Perfect:	"No, not pepper pizza. The correct name is pepperoni pizza, but that's okay. I could still understand you. I tell you what, we'll practice pronouncing your spelling word tomorrow evening. Remember, P E P P E R O N I spells pepperoni."
Rebelling:	"Why don't you B U Z Z O F F? I'm tired of listening to all of your garbage. This is not school. And you're not the teacher. Even school isn't this boring."
Clowning:	"He's boring. He's boring. He's got us all snoring. Yuk, yuk, yuk. Boring and snoring." (*Make a loud snoring sound.*)
Quiet:	(*Frown and hide behind others.*)
Talking A Lot:	"Hey, look at this. Here's a pint of Sno White's booze. Alcohol is not a good thing for you. It was invented back in Egypt around 3000 B.C. Jimmy Brum once drank alcohol and it made him barf. Each state has laws against drunk driving, and it is not good for kids to drink, but I really think that . . ."
Perfect:	"Wait. What should we do? Let's pour all the vodka down the sink. Then we'll fill the empty bottle with water. We can put it right back where we found it. Everyone will pretend like nothing's happened."

Rebelling: "I have a better idea. Let's drink the booze. We'll show Sno White. We can get drunk instead of her. Let's do it."

Crying: "Sob, sob, sob." (*Make a low-pitched crying sound.*)

Blaming: "Now look at what you've done. She's crying all over again. It's all your fault. Again. You scared her."

**Talking
A Lot:**   "Suzie and Billy had a big fight at school yesterday. Mrs. Robins sent them to the Principal's office. Have you noticed more kids getting in trouble at school lately? Why do you suppose . . .?"

Perfect: "Here comes Sno White."

Rebelling: "Let's split."

Chorus:
"Oh no, oh no, the alcoholic woes (*whistle*) oh no, oh no, oh no.
Oh no, oh no, the drug abuse woes (*whistle*) oh no, oh no, oh no.
Oh no, oh no, the alcoholic woes (*whistle*) oh no, oh no, oh no.

Oh no."

Line Of Defense

(Ages 6 and up)

With this game, children have the opportunity not only to become aware of their defenses, but also to explore their feelings. By discovering that their peers also mask feelings with defenses, children strengthen their emotional bonds with others.

Description

Four children brainstorm as many defenses as possible and list them on the board. The children individually choose a defense and then form a line. Taking turns (or simultaneously if the group has experience) they use facial expressions and body language to "mime" the defense they have chosen. The "audience" guesses what defense each child is using.

Once the defense(s) have been guessed, the children share a time when they used this particular defense and describe the hidden feelings (the "defended stuff").

Example

The facilitator whispered the word "clowning" into the ear of each player. The audience waited, but not for long. Johnny held his sides, doubling over in mouth-agape mime laughter; Julie jumped jerkily up and down flailing her arms; Terry stood rigid with eyes straight ahead while making contorted funny faces; Robert stuck out his tongue at the group while crossing his eyes.

The audience quickly broke into laughter and shouted, "Clowning!" Each child then described a time he or she had used this defense to hide a feeling. One child in the audience jumped on a table and danced around. Instead of admonishing his behavior, the facilitator asked Ryan what defense he was using. He didn't respond, so she turned to the group and asked, "What do you see as Ryan's defense, and what feelings may be underneath?" Molly said, "Rebelling." The group agreed. Different children guessed the underlying feelings — lonely, angry or nervous. Paula pinpointed it by saying, "Maybe he just wants some attention." A few weeks later Ryan admitted to the group that no one listens to him at home.

Affirmations

- "You don't have to act out to get my attention."
- "Know your defenses well, and you'll get to know the feelings underneath."
- "Defenses are important to have. You can choose when you want to take them down, and get closer to other people and yourself."

Comments

- This exercise helps children understand other people's actions and emotions, as well as their own. This step is essential in learning to separate and detach, when necessary, from what others say and do.
- This game opens the door to the spontaneous, magical child who has been lost and obscured.

Defense Mate

(Ages 10 and up)

This game is a good follow-up to Sno White and the Seven Defenses or to a mini-lecture and discussion on defenses. Like Sno White it explores a variety of defenses to help children become aware of their own. It's especially effective with children 10 and over, but, with extra direction and support, it also works with younger kids. A large open space helps facilitate this game.

Description

An even number of children stand in a circle. Each child is given an index card with instructions not to let others see it. On each card is written a defense such as clowning, blaming, perfect, quiet or withdrawn. Each defense must be held by two separate children. The facilitators make sure each child can identify the defense on his or her card and give clues about how to act out that particular defense.

When everyone is ready, the facilitators shout, "One, two, three, go!" The children walk around the room silently acting out their defense through facial expressions, body language and other nonverbal communications. As they act each kid tries to find the other person acting out the same defense. Once they have found their "defense-mate," they lock arms and walk together. They tell the facilitator which defense they represent, and hand in their index cards. The game continues until each person has found his or her defense mate. A discussion on defenses follows.

Example

In playing Defense Mates children walked around the room in a variety of poses. Sally with a very stern look on her face kept pointing a finger at the other children. Jimmy sat in the corner, his hands covering his face. George walked around holding his stomach as if he were laughing. Laura kept punching and kicking at the air. She looked very angry. Two by two, children recognized their defense mate and locked arms. Two kids remained unpaired. Jimmy was still sitting in the corner, covering his face; close by, Gloria was doing the same thing. Neither had looked out from their withdrawal to recognize the other.

Affirmations

- "Your defenses are okay, particularly if you choose when to use them."
- "You can have fun and take good care of yourself at the same time."

Comments

- This activity takes very little time, so play it several times allowing the children ample opportunity to act out a variety of defenses.
- Process after each round. Ask how they felt using the assigned defense, whether or not they use this defense in their daily lives, and what defenses they tend to use the most.
- Stress again that defenses are okay — they are neither good nor bad.

Materials

- Two sets of index cards with a defense written on each card. (The total number of defenses used must be half the number of children participating.)

5

Problem Solving

Growing up in a chemically dependent family can be a nightmare for children. Broken promises, verbal violence, mixed messages, parental inconsistencies, threat of abuse, unsafe touch and neglect are some of the problems they may endure. Parents aren't always available or able to meet their children's needs in a consistent way. Many kids don't know what normal is because they constantly readjust to chaos and craziness. These kids often end up isolated in silence and pain.

However, children can learn to recognize and solve many of the problems they encounter. They can learn to choose healthier ways of responding to people and situations. Facilitators can offer children a variety of healthy coping behaviors. It is important to teach them practical tools to solve problems. At the top of the list is asking for help. They can learn about many people in the community who will help them, and that it's okay to ask for help. Coming to believe this, children understand that they need never be alone again. Above all, children learn how essential it is to take good care of themselves — to always stay safe. They must learn to put themselves first.

Games

1. **12 Steps For Kids**

2. **Wheel Of Misfortune**

3. **Many People Can Help Me**

4. **Problem Box, Solution Box**

59

12 Steps For Kids

1. I am powerless over alcohol, drugs and other people's behavior, and my life got real messed up because of it.

2. I need help. I can't do it alone anymore.

3. I've made a decision to reach out for a Power greater than me to help out.

4. I wrote down all the things that bother me about myself and others, and all the things I like, too.

5. I shared these with someone I trust because I don't have to keep them a secret anymore.

6. My Higher Power helps me with this, too.

7. The more I trust myself and my Higher Power, the more I learn to trust others.

8. I made a list of the people I hurt and the ways I hurt myself. I can now forgive myself and others.

9. I talked with these people even if I was scared to because I knew that it would help me feel better about myself.

10. I keep on discovering more things about myself each day and if I hurt someone, I apologize.

11. When I am patient and pray, I get closer to my Higher Power, and that helps me to know myself better.

12. By using these steps, I've become a new person. I don't have to feel alone anymore, and I can help others.

12 Steps For Kids

(Ages 7 and up)

While the 12 Steps For Kids underlie the entire recovery program for young children of alcoholics, they are especially useful for problem solving. It is not surprising that the time-tested 12 Steps practiced by AA, Al-Anon, OA and other 12-Step programs are also helpful for kids in their daily lives.

Description

In formulating the 12 Steps for kids we changed the "we" to "I" because they need to learn to switch the focus to themselves and their individual concerns. There is no single prescribed way to employ the steps. The important thing is to encourage and guide children in using them. Ask the kids to name specific problems that are troubling them and list them on the board.

Each week (or day if the group is meeting daily) discuss three of the steps in relation to the list. Identify problems that are amenable to solution or assistance by working the steps under discussion. Talk about applying the steps to certain problems. Also, during some of the other games, as feelings and frustrations surface, kids can discover how the steps may be applied. Some groups will be able to sustain discussion of the steps longer than others. Be flexible. The kids often come up with their own creative ideas about how to use the steps.

Example

A group of young children had just finished the bicycle game during which they had quickly experienced the calmer, pre-addiction phase, the addiction phase and the loss of control. When asked what step or steps were related to their experience, they said, "The first step. At the end we were powerless." In the ensuing discussion about solutions, they realized that their need for help was closely related to the second step. "I need help. I'm not alone any more."

Affirmation

- "You can learn and grow and be yourself by following the 12 Steps."

Comments

- The 12 Steps are the path to recovery.
- Each time children utilize the steps in a manner that helps them solve a problem or bring some serenity to their lives, they will have made significant progress in their recovery.

Wheel Of Misfortune

(Ages 6 and up)

We have found that children love this game. It involves cooperation and teamwork in solving the real-life problems found in
alcoholic families. Children come to see that they have choices and
options in handling tough situations. It also prepares them to handle
any similar real-life crisis in the future. While this is a game children
of all ages enjoy, "The Wheel of Misfortune" is particularly effective
with 6- to 12-year-olds. Time flies when kids play this game.

Description

The facilitators divide children into groups of three, and each
group selects a team name. With a spin of the wheel (see Figure 6)
each team lands on a particular letter of the alphabet. The team looks
at the "Wheel of Misfortune" gameboard to identify its problem, e.g.,
driving with a drunk parent or being embarrassed by a drinking
parent in the presence of one's friends (see Figure 7). The team
brainstorms a variety of ways to solve the dilemma.

Facilitators emphasize the importance of taking good care of
yourself and always staying safe. When all groups are ready, each
team presents its findings to the large group. Discussion ensues.

64

Example

Bobby, Jeremy and Lori, all 9 years old, called their team "The Cool Cats." With a spin of the wheel they found Mom passed out on the living room rug. What to do? The suggestions flew back and forth — some silly, some outrageous, others ingenious. Bobby suggested that they go get a neighbor. Lori wanted to call 911. Jeremy said, "It's a good idea to try and wake Mom first." They finally agreed to do all three — try and revive Mom, call 911 for an ambulance and then get a neighbor. They were met with cheers and clapping when they shared with the larger group.

Affirmations

- "You can make helpful choices in your life."
- "It's good to take care of yourself."

Comments

- Play the game over and over to allow each team to brainstorm ways of handling a variety of problem situations. This helps them believe they truly have choices in their lives.
- This game is best used in conjunction with "Many People Can Help Me."
- Above all this is an activity that stresses trust and cooperation among the children. The key here is teamwork. Everyone wins.

Materials

- Spinning Wheel
- "Wheel of Misfortune" gameboard

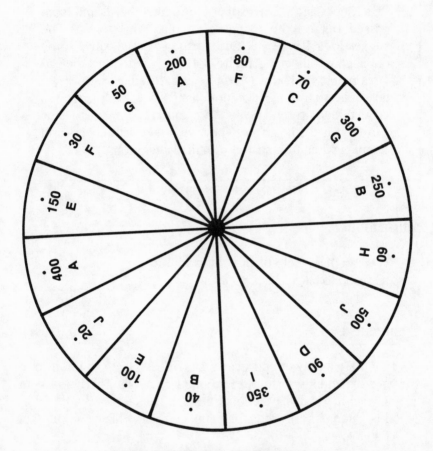

Figure 6. The Wheel of Misfortune

A   Unsafe touch

B   Yelled at for no reason

C   Passed out on the floor

D   Driving with a drunk parent

E   Mom or Dad not coming home

F   Watching parent getting beat-up

G   Brother or sister getting hit

H   Asked if you want alcohol or drugs

I   Embarrassed with friends

J   Stuck in the middle

Figure 7. Wheel of Misfortune Gameboard

Many People Can Help Me

(Ages 9 and up)

This is an extremely important activity that provides children with a list of important phone numbers that they can use when they need help. Compiling the list in the company of other kids emphasizes the importance of having such a list. Stress that these numbers are used by other kids with similar problems. It's fun to work on this activity while everyone is sprawled on the floor with a lot of space for legs and elbows. Play some of the children's favorite music softly in the background. This activity works best with children over the age of 9. Younger children require additional support and assistance from the group facilitators.

Description

Place telephone books, pencils and "Many People Can Help Me" worksheets (see Figure 8) on the floor. Encourage the children to find a comfortable place on the floor with plenty of room. Give each child a worksheet and stress that there are many people who can help them if they need it. The group brainstorms a variety of people they could turn to for help — Aunt Betty, the police, family doctor, their group leader, Grandpa and others.

When many possibilities have been mentioned, the children take pencils and complete the worksheets. They list people they'd feel comfortable in calling if they needed help. If they don't know the person's number, they look it up. The facilitators assist children individually by suggesting other people the kids might call and helping them use the phone book. The activity is over when everyone has at least five names and telephone numbers on their worksheet. Facilitators encourage children to keep their worksheet in a safe, easily accessible place in case they ever need it in a hurry.

Example

During this game Annie put the facilitator's phone numbers on her list. Annie completed the group and moved to a distant city. Eight months later she called her facilitator long distance in the middle of the night. She had awakened to find her mom passed out on the kitchen floor with empty liquor and pill bottles beside her. Annie thought her mom was dead, but somehow she remembered her list. By calling her facilitator, Annie got help for her mom because the facilitator called long distance for an ambulance. Annie saved her mother's life.

Affirmations

- "You can make helpful choices in your life."
- "You are not alone — there are lots of people who can help."
- "It's okay to ask for help."

Comments

- This activity is especially effective when combined with the "Wheel of Misfortune" game.
- Children often ask one another for their telephone numbers to include on their lists. This has been the start of many friendships.

Materials

- Local telephone books
- Pencils
- "Many People Can Help Me" List

Figure 8. "Many People Can Help Me" List

Name   **Phone Number**

_____

_____

_____

_____

_____

_____

_____

_____

_____

_____

Name   **Phone Number**

_____

_____

_____

_____

_____

_____

_____

_____

_____

_____

_____

Problem Box, Solution Box

(Ages 6 and up)

This powerful activity helps young children see that their problems are not unique, especially the alcoholism in the family. Kids share their own problems with the group, the feelings involved and the ways they deal positively with them. This activity particularly works well for 6- to 12-year-olds with some variations for their different developmental abilities. We have frequently used this activity during weekend retreats.

Description

This activity is best done in a wide, open space where children can sit comfortably on the floor. Spread colored markers, crayons and index cards on the floor. Allow children to find a space for themselves with lots of room. After a brief discussion of the problems often faced when growing up with alcoholism, the facilitators pass out index cards. Using colored markers or crayons, children draw or write about problems in their own lives on the index cards. Facilitators emphasize that they don't have to write their names on the cards. This allows kids to draw or write about a problem that they might not otherwise have been willing to share.

When all are finished, they put their cards into a large wooden problem box. After the box is shaken well, each child pulls out a card. In turn they read or describe the problem on the card they have chosen. The group brainstorms ways to solve the problem. Children tell how they've solved similar problems in their own lives. The "active" child writes or draws a couple of possible solutions on the back of the card. Once thoroughly discussed, the card is placed in the Solution Box.

Example

Sue picked a card out of the Problem Box and read the problem — "Dad never gives me any attention."

Ten-year-old Bobby said that he had written the card. He was happy his dad didn't drink anymore, but was still sad that he didn't get much time with his father. Bobby said, "I wish we could do things together, but Dad's always working or going to AA meetings. It's not fair."

Others in the group shared similar experiences. Gloria suggested that Bobby write his dad a note inviting him to spend a special day with Bobby at the park. "Let your dad know how much it means to you to spend time alone with him." Sue wrote this on the index card and put it in the Solution Box. Although skeptical, Bobby wrote the letter to his dad. Two weeks later he reported in group about the great day he had with his father.

Affirmations

- "It's okay to ask others for what you need."
- "You are special."
- "You are worth receiving special treatment."
- "Your friends can give you a lot of help."

Comments

- Facilitators play a crucial role in helping kids to discriminate between safe and unsafe solutions to various problems.
- In exploring various options, children get in touch with resources they may turn to. Above all, the children work together, supporting each other along the way.

Materials

- Two wooden boxes (cigar boxes work well)
- Placards saying "Problem Box" and "Solution Box"
- Colored markers
- Crayons
- Index cards

Self-Esteem/Celebrate Me

Children are beautiful creatures; yet living with alcoholism and drug addiction can make them feel entirely alone and disconnected from their family, others and self. It is extremely difficult for these children to appreciate their own beauty. The games in this section help children develop a greater appreciation of themselves and others. Moreover, by coming to see and feel the bonds between people, children "get" that they no longer need to be alone. These games provide insights while simultaneously allowing the "kid" to flourish. They help us all, young and old alike, to get in touch with the magic of childhood — the spontaneity, creativity, joy, wonder, laughter and play.

During this journey of celebration, children learn that everyone has special qualities, including their chemically dependent parents. They realize that they can change how they feel about themselves, and that it's okay to feel good about their accomplishments. More importantly, they begin to understand that it's okay to feel good about who they are as people. That is the essence of *Kids' Power*. When *Kids' Power* turns on, children can celebrate their part in this wonderful universe.

Games

1. **All About Me**

2. **Living Cards**

3. **Like-Alike Game**

4. **My Secret Pal**

All About Me

(Ages 3 and up)

This exercise helps children understand that they are important, loving, caring and valuable young people. It also helps them further release the denial and delusion that pervades the alcoholic family.

Description

Children gather in a large circle. The facilitator, using a microphone, interviews each child as a "special guest star." The interviewer asks each child his or her name and age, the name and relationship of family members who are chemically dependent, and the names and ages of any other family members. The interviewer also asks them to disclose something they do like and something they don't like about themselves. It's crucial for the facilitator to offer affirmations for the child's progress in his or her own recovery.

Some examples are: "I'm glad you're here," "You deserve to be here," "You're learning to know who you are," "You've pushed and tested limits and that's okay," "You've explored who you are," "You've taken many healthy risks in the group," "You've learned to be responsible for your own needs," "You've grown a lot," and "You're a unique and special person."

Each interview is celebrated by those in the studio audience who cheer and clap at every statement the "guest star" makes.

Affirmations

- "You deserve to be here."
- "You're learning to know who you are."
- "You've taken many risks in the group."

Comments

- These affirmations (as part of the interview process) are just a few of many that can be used. Learn more and practice them. They help children immensely when appropriately used.
- You might want to audio or video tape the process for later viewing or to add glamour to the occasion. This also gives children an opportunity to see how others view them, thereby helping them develop and accept their own identity. Assure the children that such a tape will be kept confidential. Please ask and get their permission to tape these proceedings if you choose this option.

Living Cards

(Ages 8 and up)

This is a powerful exercise in peer affirmation. It is incredibly helpful in promoting self-esteem. If at all possible, do this exercise on the floor. Each child will need a tablet to write on. But kids get more out of "Living Cards" if they sprawl across the room. Play some of their favorite music softly in the background.

Description

Have the children find places on the floor with plenty of room. Give each of them two pieces of white paper (8½ x 11 inches). Spread crayons, colored markers and pencils across the floor. Have the children write just their name in the middle of the page. Encourage them to be creative with different colors and specialized lettering (e.g., block or script). Then ask them to reflect silently on the *special qualities* everyone contributes to the group. No one does any writing yet. (Since the kids have been with one another for a few weeks in group this shouldn't be difficult.) The facilitators can provide a few examples to help people get the idea.

After a few minutes, the children pass their paper to the left, and their neighbors write briefly about the special qualities of the person whose name is on the sheet. This continues until each paper goes around the group and comes back to the owner. Take time for each group member to absorb all the special things written about him or her. Then everyone has a chance to share his or her Living Card with the others. Ask how each child feels about the comments on his or her card. Children may take their Living Cards home. Many hang them in their rooms; others have them framed.

Example

At the first Kids' Kamp, 10-year-old Steven was having a rough time. He believed he couldn't do anything right and didn't fit in. He wanted to go home. During the "Living Cards" exercise, others wrote about his courage, swimming ability and friendliness. When Steven read his card, he lit up like a Christmas tree. He came to see himself in a new way. His eyes filled with tears when he told the group, "Thanks, I guess I really am okay."

Affirmations

- "Everyone has special qualities."
- "You are a beautiful and special person."
- "It's okay to feel good about yourself."

Comments

- This activity works with younger kids if the facilitators write for them. A variation on this theme is to have the little ones draw a picture of what's special about the others — a flower, the sunshine, a rainbow or a favorite toy.
- Despite concern that group members might write derogatory things to one another, we have rarely seen this. The facilitators must set the tone for this exercise by sharing, and they also must participate with their own card.

Materials

- White paper
- Crayons
- Colored pencils/markers
- Tablets of paper

Like-Alike Game

(Ages 7 and up)

This is another self-esteem exercise that builds on "Living Cards." It sharpens and encourages children's ability to perceive positive attributes within themselves. This game helps children understand that they are worthwhile and important human beings who can and should acknowledge their own goodness.

Description

Sitting in a circle, the kids take turns finishing the statement: "What I like about me is . . ." The circle is completed three times. Then they go around twice again, first clockwise, then counterclockwise, saying: "What I like about you is . . ." Some children have difficulty finding something they like about themselves. It may help to encourage them to look at their behavior in the group or at play. Or, the facilitator may say, "It's very easy for me to see many things." Children usually respond to this and will find something special about themselves.

This exercise generally warms up the second and third time around. The children become more intense, self-disclosing and spontaneous. When they are doing "What I like about you . . .," ask the children to share something meaningful they have recently discovered about the other person. Try to discourage statements such as: "I like your hair, shirt, dress, etc." If prodded a little, they usually respond.

Example

One of the most feeling responses from one child to another was, "I like the way you're good to yourself." Both children were age 9.

Affirmation

- "You can always find your own special qualities if you honestly look for them."

Comments

- This game helps children break through learned shame and guilt.
- Kids begin to understand that open and positive communication with peers is healthier than constantly acting out their defenses.

My Secret Pal

(Ages 6 and up)

This simple game can stimulate powerful sharing by group members. It facilitates group closeness and bonding. All age groups enjoy this activity, but 6- to 12-year-olds especially. This game works best when used in conjunction with another activity such as "All About Me" or "Living Cards."

Description

Each child's name is written on a 3x5-inch card. The cards are scattered across a table, written side down. The children select a card from the table and keep the name on the card a secret. The name on the card is their secret pal. The children are told to carefully watch their secret pals during the session without being too obvious about it. Near the end of the meeting while other activities are completed, the children guess the identity of the person who has been watching them. That person comes forward and shares something special about his or her pal. The facilitators may participate in this game.

Example

Kevin, age 9, had been coming to group for a year. He had made good progress, but his constant put-downs made it clear he was his own worst enemy. Kevin's secret pal turned out to be Joe, the most popular member of the group. Joe was well-liked, always seemed to have the right answers and was a great athlete. When his turn came Joe said, "Kevin, I look up to you because you are kind and strong. You were nice to me when I first came here. You made me feel welcome. You say what you think. I wish I could do that. I get scared to disagree. That's what's special about you."

Kevin could hardly contain himself. The most popular kid in group had told him he could do something very well. Kevin smiled and left group feeling proud. He still beams today when he talks about that group. It made a crucial difference to him and helped develop his self-esteem.

Affirmations

- "You are a special, beautiful person."
- "You have special qualities."
- "It's okay to feel good about yourself."

Comments

- It's important for the facilitators to participate in this activity. They may help set the tone for this process.
- An option is to follow-up with a brief discussion on how we are all special. Cap this off with a group song or special treat.

Materials

- Index cards

Appendix A

Sources of information for and about young children of alcoholics

Books And Pamphlets

Ackerman, R. J. **Children of Alcoholics: A Bibliography and Resources Guide.** Pompano Beach, FL: Health Communications, 1987.

Ackerman, R. J. **Children of Alcoholics: A Guidebook for Educators, Therapists, and Parents.** Holmes Beach, FL: Learning Publications, 1978.

Alateen — Hope for Children of Alcoholics. New York: Al-Anon Family Group Headquarters, 1980.

Black, C. **It Will Never Happen to Me.** Denver, CO: Medical Administration, 1982.

Black, C. **My Dad Loves Me — My Dad Has a Disease.** Newport Beach, CA: ACT, 1979.

Black, C. **Repeat After Me.** Denver, CO: Medical Administration, 1985.

Brooks, C. **The Secret Everyone Knows.** San Diego, CA: Operation Cork, 1981.

Clark, K. K. **Grow Deep Not Just Tall.** St. Paul, MN: CEP, 1984.

Clark, K. K. **Where Have All the Children Gone.** St. Paul, MN: CEP, 1977.

Clarke, J. I. **Self-Esteem: A Family Affair.** Minneapolis, MN: Winston Press, 1978.

Cork, M. **The Forgotten Children.** Toronto, Canada: Addiction Research Foundation, 1969.

Deutsch, C. **Broken Bottles, Broken Dreams.** New York: Teachers College Press, 1982.

DiGiovanni, K. **My House Is Different.** Center City, MN: Hazelden, 1986.

Figueroa, R. **Pablito's Secret.** Pompano Beach, FL: Health Communications, 1984.

Fluegelman, A. (ed.). **The New Games Book.** Garden City, NY: Dolphin Books, 1976.

Foston-English, M. **Kids Are Special Curriculum.** Cupertino, CA, 1985.

Goldberg, L. **Counseling for Children of Alcoholics.** Tallahassee, FL: Apalachee Community Mental Health Services, 1983.

Hastings, J., and Typpo, M. **An Elephant in the Living Room.** Minneapolis, MN: CompCare Publications, 1984.

Hornik, E. **You and Your Alcoholic Parent**. New York: Associated Press, 1974.

Jones, P. **The Brown Bottle**. Center City, MN: Hazelden, 1982.

Lerner, R., and Naditch, B. **Children Are People Support Group Training Manual**. Children Are People. St. Paul, MN: 1984.

Melquist, E. **Pepper**. New York: National Council on Alcoholism, 1974.

Morehouse, E., and Scola, C. **Children of Alcoholics: Meeting the Needs of the Young CoAs in the School Setting**. South Laguna, CA: National Association for Children of Alcoholics, 1986.

Oppenheimer, J. **Francesca, Baby**. New York: Scholastic Book Services, 1976.

Ryerson, E. **When Your Parent Drinks Too Much: A Book for Teenagers**. New York: Facts on File, 1985.

Seixas, J. **Alcohol: What It Is, What It Does**. New York: Greenwillow Books, 1977.

Seixas, J. **Living With a Parent Who Drinks Too Much**. New York: Greenwillow Books, 1979.

Snyder, A. **First Step**. New York: Holt, Rinehart & Winston, 1975.

Wegscheider-Cruse, S. **Another Chance: Hope and Health for the Alcoholic Family**. Palo Alto, CA: Science & Behavior Books, 1981.

Wegscheider-Cruse, S. **The Family Trap**. Minneapolis, MN: Nurturing Networks, 1979.

What's Drunk Mama. New York: Al-Anon Family Group Headquarters, 1977.

Films

A Story about Feelings, Johnson Institute, 510 First Avenue North, Minneapolis, MN 55441.

All Bottled Up, AIMS Media Inc., 626 Hustin Avenue, Glendale, CA 91201.

Children of Denial (with Claudia Black), MAC Publishing, 5005 East 39th Avenue, Denver, CO 80207.

Francesca, Baby, Walt Disney Educational Media Company, 500 South Buena Vista Street, Burbank, CA 91521.

Hope for the Children, Health Communications, 3201 SW 15th Street, Deerfield Beach, FL 33442.

Knowing, Feeling, Growing: Rational Emotive Therapy for Children of Alcoholics, Wentworth Quast, PhD, University of Minnesota, Program in Health Care, Psychology, Division of Community Health Services, Minneapolis, MN 55455.

Lots of Kids Like Us, Gerald T. Rogers Productions, 5225 Old Orchard Road, Suite #23A, Skokie, IL 60077.

She Drinks a Little, Learning Corporation of America, 1350 Avenue of the Americas, New York, NY 10019.

Soft Is the Heart of a Child, Operation Cork, 8939 Villa La Jolla Drive, San Diego, CA 92037.

The Summer We Moved to Elm Street, McGraw-Hill Films, 330 West 42nd Street, New York, NY 10036.

Appendix B

National Resources

National Association for Children of Alcoholics
    31582 Coast Highway, Suite B
    South Laguna, CA 92677
    (714) 499-3889
    Advocacy, Information, Education and Resources for Children of Alcoholics

Children of Alcoholics Foundation, Inc.
    31st Floor
    200 Park Avenue
    New York, New York 10166
    (212) 351-2680

Other Books By . . .

HEALTH COMMUNICATIONS, INC.

Enterprise Center
3201 Southwest 15th Street
Deerfield Beach, FL 33442
Phone: 800-851-9100

ADULT CHILDREN OF ALCOHOLICS
Janet Woititz
Over a year on The New York Times Best Seller list,this book is the primer on Adult Children of Alcoholics.
ISBN 0-932194-15-X $6.95

STRUGGLE FOR INTIMACY
Janet Woititz
Another best seller, this book gives insightful advice on learning to love more fully.
ISBN 0-932194-25-7 $6.95

DAILY AFFIRMATIONS: For Adult Children of Alcoholics
Rokelle Lerner
These positive affirmations for every day of the year paint a mental picture of your life as you choose it to be.
ISBN 0-932194-27-3 $6.95

CHOICEMAKING: For Co-dependents, Adult Children and Spirituality Seekers — Sharon Wegscheider-Cruse
This useful book defines the problems and solves them in a positive way.
ISBN 0-932194-26-5 $9.95

LEARNING TO LOVE YOURSELF: Finding Your Self-Worth
Sharon Wegscheider-Cruse
"Self-worth is a choice, not a birthright", says the author as she shows us how we can choose positive self-esteem.
ISBN 0-932194-39-7 $7.95

LET GO AND GROW: Recovery for Adult Children
Robert Ackerman
An in-depth study of the different characteristics of adult children of alcoholics with guidelines for recovery.
ISBN 0-932194-51-6 $8.95

LOST IN THE SHUFFLE: The Co-dependent Reality
Robert Subby
A look at the unreal rules the co-dependent lives by and the way out of the dis-eased reality.
ISBN 0-932194-45-1 $8.95